GUIDE WITH RECONSTRUCTIONS

POMPEII HERCULANEUM

past and present

PAST & PRESENT®

Text by **A. DE FRANCISCIS** with revision by **I. BRAGANTINI**
Drawings and reconstructions: Vision s.r.l.
Layout: U.Ulivieri

Copyright © 1996 by VISION S.r.l.
Via Livorno, 20 – 00162 Roma – Tel/Fax (39) 06 44292688 E-Mail : Vision.srl@stm.it

ISBN 88- 8162-007-3

Printed in Italy by Tipolitografica CS - Padova

POMPEII
ITS LIFE AND HISTORY

Pompeii stands on a lava spur running out into the plain from the slopes of Vesuvius, a short distance from the sea and from the river Sarno. The site was well suited for human settlement, of an agricultural and commercial character, and was probably already inhabited from an early date, when Campania was still occupied by the Oscans. In early historical times the context of the relations with the neighbouring greek colonies became very complex, in particular with Cuma, as well as with the Etruscan world, which on several occasions clashed with the Greeks in an attempt to oust them from the control of this region. Pompeii was involved in the invasion and subsequent domination of Campania by the Samnites (about 424 B.C.), and from this moment on we are better informed about the lay-out and development of the city. It was, however, only a small place, and mentions of it in the history of the following centuries are correspondingly few.

During the Samnite wars it repelled an attack by a Roman naval raiding party, but with the establishment of peace it entered the Roman orbit as an allied city, an alliance to which it remained faithful even during the dark days of the Carthaginian invasion under Hannibal. Throughout this period Pompeii kept its commercial independence, its own magistrates and language; then, in the Social war, it became involved on the side of the Italic allies and in 89 B.C. it was besieged, stormed and subjected by Sulla. In 80 it was settled as a Roman colony under the name of *Colonia Cornelia Veneria Pompeiorum*. Henceforth its history is part of the larger picture of Roman history. The only local episode of note, mentioned by Tacitus, is a riot in the amphitheatre between the inhabitants of Pompeii and Nuceria (A.D. 59), which led to the suspension of all spectacles for a period of ten years.

Pompeii was badly damaged by the earthquake which hit Campania in A.D. 62 and the damage had not all been repaired when, in 79, an eruption of Vesuvius killed many of the inhabitants and buried the whole city beneath a rain of ash and cinders. A graphic description of the disaster is given in two letters by Pliny the Younger to Tacitus, describing among other things the rescue work undertaken by his uncle, Pliny the Elder, who was at the time commander of the Roman fleet at Misenum and who paid for his generous initiative with his life.

Pompeii never rose from its ruins and the site was virtually abandoned. The first signs of the buried city came to light between 1594 and 1600, when the architect Domenico Fontana cut a channel for the waters of the river Sarno; but on that occasion the exploration was not followed up. Then, in 1748, regular excavations were started by the king of Naples, Charles of Bourbon, and they have continued without a break ever since.

During this long time methods of excavations have of course changed. At first the search was only for sculpture, paintings, mosaics and other objects of artistic interest or curiosity, and the ruins themselves were often reburied. With time, however, thanks to a steady improvement of excavation methods and an increasing interest in the vestiges of the past, the remains were systematically explored and studied in all their manifold aspects, and every effort was made to preserve and to restore them.

The object of the more recent excavations has been to present the houses and streets of Pompeii as they were, and to afford the visitor as complete a vision as possible of an ancient city. Mention may be made of the technique introduced by the great archaeologist, Giuseppe Fiorelli, whereby the shapes of buried organic features (human bodies, trees, wooden objects) are recovered by pouring plaster into the impressions left by their dissolution. Thanks to the exceptional circumstances of the burial of Pompeii (and of course of Herculaneum), where life suddenly came to an end in the space of two days, the excavator can reap a rich harvest, not only of the sort of remains which one can find in any part of the ancient world, but also of all sorts of objects, furniture and other items of daily life which elsewhere are apt to be scattered and destroyed. Here for example one can study in a wealth of varied examples the development of the

Battle between the Pompeians and their neighbours of Nuceria

5

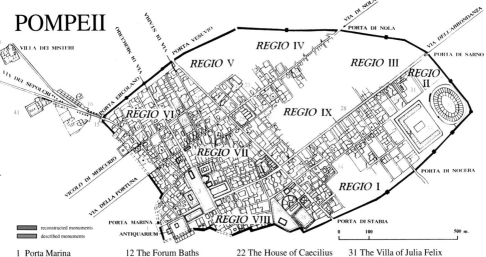

POMPEII

VILLA DEI MISTERI

VIA DEL SEPOLCRI

REGIO V
REGIO IV
REGIO III
REGIO II
REGIO VI
REGIO IX
REGIO VII
REGIO I
REGIO VIII

VIA DI MERCURIO
VIA IS TI VIA
PORTA VESUVIO
VIA DI NOLA
PORTA DI NOLA
VIA DELL'ABBONDANZA
PORTA DI SARNO
PORTA ERCOLANO
VICOLO DI MERCURIO
VIA DELLA FORTUNA
VIA DELL'ABBONDANZA
PORTA DI NOCERA
PORTA MARINA
ANTIQUARIUM
PORTA DI STABIA

reconstructed monuments
described monuments

0   100   500 m.

1 Porta Marina
2 Temple of Venus
3 The Forum
4 The Temple of Apollo
5 The Basilica
6 The Comitium
7 The Eumachia Building
8 The Temple of Vespasian
9 The Shrine of the Lares
10 The Macellum
11 The Temple of Fortuna Augusta

12 The Forum Baths
13 The House of the Tragic Poet
14 The House of Sallust
15 The Herculaneum Gate
16 The Street of the Tombs
17 The House of Meleager
18 The House of Large Fountain
19 The House of Faun
20 The House of Vettii
21 The House of the Golden Cupids

22 The House of Caecilius Jucundus
23 The House of the Silver Wedding
24 The House of Centenary
25 The Central Baths
26 Pistrinium
27 The Stabian Baths
28 Via dell'Abbondanza
29 The House of Octavius Quartio
30 The House of the Venus

31 The Villa of Julia Felix
32 The Amphitheatre
33 The Palaestra
34 The House of Menander
35 The Temple of Isis
36 The Triangular Forum
37 The Theatre
38 The Porticus post scaenam
39 The Odeon
40 The Villa of Mysteries
41 The Villa of Diomede

Italic and Roman house and of its painted decoration from the 2nd century B.C. to the 1st century A.D.

The wall-paintings can be classified according to their style into four main groups, a classification which is based on decorative systems that can be dated within certain limits, and which is valid also for other archaeological sites that are less well documented. Another valuable contribution to knowledge is that which the scratched and painted inscriptions of Pompeii make to the history of manners, institutions and the spoken language of the Roman world in the 1st century A.D.

In the final phase of the city, as one sees it today, it was surrounded by walls with defensive towers and gates. There were two main streets running east and west (*decumani*), the Via di Nola and the Via dell'Abbondanza, and one north and south (*cardo*), the Via di Stabia. The other roads mostly ran parallel to these. The city-centre, the Forum, lay towards the south-west, with other centres of public life around the Triangular Forum and the Amphiteatre.

PORTA MARINA AND VILLA SUBURBANA

The Porta Marina dates from the 2nd century B.C. and is one of the best preserved of the several gates that open through the city-walls of Pompeii. It faces towards the sea, whence its name; and although the road through it is rather too steep for comfort, it affords the most direct link between the hill on which Pompeii stands and the coastal plain. Inside the gate the road, under the name of the Via Marina, passes between the Temple of Venus, the Basilica and the Temple of Apollo and leads straight to the city-centre, the Forum. The gate is spanned by a single barrel vault, within which are two passage-ways: that on the left, up steps, for foot passengers, that on the right, somewhat less steep, for pack-animals; it was probably too steep for vehicles. The passages were closed by double doors. With the establishment of peace, under Augustus, the walls lost their military purpose and a villa was built up against the outer face, to the right of the Gate. The part so far excavated includes a long portico wing opening on to a dining hall with Third Style paintings and a group of other rooms. In front of it, spreading over the line of the early road leading up to the Gate, was a large garden.

TEMPLE OF VENUS

Dominating the plain below, and formerly surrounded by a wall of reticulate masonry, is the sacred precinct of Venus, the protecting divinity of Pompeii. In the middle is the temple podium, and here and there are traces of the earlier buildings that were demolished to make way for the sanctuary. The temple was adorned with marble, and the character of the surviving remains indicates a considerable degree of opulence; but it was badly damaged in the earthquake of 62, and it was still in ruins when it was overwhelmed by the eruption.

THE FORUM *(REG. VII)*

Along the south side were three large halls, richly decorated in marble, no doubt intended to serve the administrative life of Pompeii. In them we can recognize the seat of the duoviri and of

The Forum: reconstruction

the aediles, the two principal magistracies, and that of the *ordo decurionum*, corresponding to our own city council.

On the west there is the main entrance of the Basilica; then, across the Via Marina and opening off it, with one side towards the Forum, the Temple of Apollo; and finally a group of buildings connected with the storage and sales of basic foodstuffs such as cereals and vegetables. It comprises the *mensa ponderaria*, the official units of measure, and a small market and storerooms.

At the north end of the piazza stands the Temple of Jupiter, picturesquely flanked by two honorary arches. This was the main city temple, built in the Samnite period and later transformed into a *Capitolium*, to house the Capitoline triad of Jupiter, Juno and Minerva. Within the lofty podium are rooms which served to house the city-treasury (*aerarium*) and the ex-voto offerings (*favissae*); a flight of steps led up to the temple proper, which had a deep Corinthian

The Forum: detail of the eastern portico

porch and a *cella* (shrine) flanked by columns. At the time of the eruption it was not yet in use after the damage incurred in the earthquake.

THE FORUM AND THE CAPITOLIUM

The centre of an ancient city was a large open space, the Forum. Around it stood the main public buildings, both civil and religious, and it was adorned with numerous monuments, serving as a setting for important ceremonial occasions and frequently also for spectacles and games. The Forum of Pompeii still preserves substantially its ancient aspect of a rectangular piazza, 124 ft. x 482 ft., running north and south, with a paving of travertine slabs and surrounded on three sides by porticoes. The porticoes are not all alike. Along the south side are parts of the original colonnade of the Samnite period, whereas the two storeys of travertine colonnades along the other two sides represent a reconstruction that was begun during the Empire, but never completed; and some buildings have porticoes of their own in front of them. Barriers prevented traffic from entering from the adjoining streets. Within the piazza stood the *suggestum* (a platform for orators)

Bronze Statue of Apollo

11

and statues erected in honour of members of the Imperial family and distinguished local citizens; but of these only the bases remain.

THE TEMPLE OF APOLLO *(REG. VII)*

The earliest traces of cult, revealed in deep excavations, go back to the 6th century B.C., but the present lay-out is of the Samnite period, with various alterations in Roman times. The precinct consists of an enclosing wall with porticoes on three sides, of which the columns were originally Ionic, carrying a Doric frieze of metopes and triglyphs. After the earthquake of 62 a facing of stucco, now destroyed, transformed the columns into Corinthian, and the frieze became continuous and was decorated with motives associated with the cult of Apollo.

To this period belong also the Fourth Style wall-paintings, with scenes from the Trojan cycle; and in front of the portico there were herms of Mercury and Maia and statues of divinities, including Apollo, Diana, Hermaphrodite and Venus. In the Augustan period the duoviri M. Holconius Rufus and C. Egnatius Postumus for 300 sesterces bought up the rights of the proprietor whose house overlooked the sanctuary from the west, raising the outer wall on this side to roof height.

The temple stood on a podium with steps in front, and inside the cella was the cult statue and a stone *omphalo*s, attribute of Apollo. The pavement was the work of the quaestor Ovius Campanus.

The altar, of Republican date and erected, as indicated by the inscription on it, by the quattuorviri on the order of the decurions, stood in the open space in front of the temple; and

beside the steps stood a column, placed there by the duoviri, L. Sepanius and M. Herennius, bearing a dedicatory inscription and carrying a sundial. It is not unlikely that the cult of Apollo was in some way associated in this temple with that also of the emperor Augustus, who had a special devotion for the god under whose protection he had won the battle of Actium in 31 B.C. against Antonius and Cleopatra.

THE BASILICA *(REG. VII)*

The Basilica lies at the south-west corner of the Forum, behind the portico. The five doors of the entrance are preceded by a vestibule, the *chalcidicum*, and there are two lesser entrances in the long sides (but that on the southern side, facing the houses of Regio VIII, was opened subsequently). Inside there is a colonnade of brick running round all four sides, of which only the lower part survives, and a responding line of two orders of half-columns along the walls. The latter are decorated in the Pompeian First Style, and at the far end stands the *tribunal,* a tall platform with a double order of superimposed columns but the pediment is the result of a mistaken restoration carried out in the twenties (1928-30). The building as a whole dates from the last decades of the 2nd century B.C., and there is an inscription of 78 B.C. scratched on one of the walls. It was wrecked by the earthquake of 62, and there is no sign of any restoration before the final catastrophe. The reconstruction that is proposed herein shows a building with a double sloping roof, that receives light from the upper floor intercolumn.

Certainly the Basilica and the Forum together constituted the centre of life and activity of the ancient city, the more so in view of the manifold mercantile interests of Pompeii. For the merchant

The Basilica: reconstruction of the interior

or banker conducting affairs, for the idler with time on his hands, for the quick-witted anxious to put his leisure to good account, for all these this was the natural place of resort.

BUILDINGS OF THE FORUM

THE COMITIUM. Another group of public buildings stood along the east side of the Forum. Starting at the south end there is the *Comitium*, with doors both from the street and from the Forum. Its function was as a place of meeting for the popular election of the magistrates.

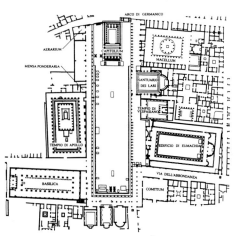

Plan of the Forum

THE EUMACHIA BUILDING, so-called after the priestess who, in the 1st century A.D.. dedicated it in her own name and that of her son, Numistrius Fronto to *Concordia Augusta* and *Pietas*. This was the seat of the guild of Fullers (*fullones*), dyers and cleaners, practising one of the most widespread of ancient crafts; it was also used for the storage and sale of stuffs. In front of it was a two-storeyed portico (*chalcidicum*) and a façade with a large marble doorway, decorated with acanthus scrollwork and flanked by four niches housing statues of Aeneas, Romulus, Augustus and Tiberius, in imitation of the Forum of Augustus in Rome. The inner courtyard had a two storeyed portico and, behind the portico, a corridor lit by windows (*cryptoporticus*). In the apse at the end must have stood the statue of Concordia Augusta, and in the corridor behind it was found the statue of Eumachia. There is a secondary entrance from the Via dell'Abbondanza.

THE so-called TEMPLE OF VESPASIAN, in front of which stands a handsome marble altar depicting a sacrificial scene, and around it, delimited by an outer wall and fronted by a portico, the sacred precinct (*templum*).

THE so-called SHRINE OF THE LARES, a spacious building once richly decorated with sculpture and marble ornament. The rear wall breaks out into an apse and in the middle stands the sacrificial altar. Though stripped of all its superficial detail, the plan is unusual and interesting. There is good reason to believe that it served as the place of worship for the *Lares publici*, the city's protecting divinities.

THE MACELLUM, a large market, the present plan of which goes back to the first century of the

The Macellum: detail of the portico

Empire. It consists of an open central area around which, opening partly inwards and partly outwards towards the street, were rows of shops. In the centre stood a circular building (*tholos*) with columns and a pool of water, and at the back a small shrine devoted to the Imperial cult, in which probably stood statues of the emperor and members of his family. (Two of these were found and are now in the Museum of Naples, but their identities are disputed).

THE TEMPLE OF FORTUNA AUGUSTA *(REG. VII)*

This dates from the closing years of the 1st century B.C. and was built, at his own expense and on his own land, by one M. Tullius, who had filled numerous public offices at Pompeii - three times duovir, quinquennalis, augur and military tribune by popular election. It was badly damaged in the earthquake of 62, and was still being rebuilt at the time of the eruption. By that date it seems already to have been for a some time in a state of decline. The flight of steps in front is interrupted by a platform at the foot, on which stood the altar (probably that reused in Flavian times for the nearby temple of Vespasian), and it was enclosed within a railing. The deep porch was carried on marble Corinthian columns and behind it the cella too was cased in marble; in the middle of the rear wall was an aedicula with colonnettes and an inscribed architrave recording the act of foundation, and along the side walls were niches for statues, two of which have survived. The temple was dedicated to Fortuna Augusta, a cult established in A.D. 3 in honour of Augustus in his capacity as "Father of his Country", and is an indication of the progressive divinization of the emperor which was already taking place under the influence of the Hellenistic courts, and which was to become increasingly important as the Empire developed. The Pompeian

The Temple of Fortuna Augusta: reconstruction

cult was in the hands of the *Ministri Fortunae Augustae,* a religious college recorded in a number of inscriptions.

Each year, on the instructions of the duoviri and aediles, the *Ministri* deposited a small statue (*signum*) in the temple. It occupied a central position, a short distance from the Forum, at the cross-roads between a street leading from the Forum and the Via di Nola. To the south of it ran a handsome portico with shops opening off it; across the street were the Forum Baths; and over the cross-roads to the north there was a honorary arch, on which stood a bronze statue, fragments of which have been recovered.

THE FORUM BATHS

The Forum Baths are of Sullan date and were built by the duovir L. Caesius and the aediles C. Occius and L. Niremius.

As was regular practice in the baths of this period, there were separate sections for men and women. The former consisted of a changing room (*apodyterium*); a circular *frigidarium*; a *tepidarium*, in which one can see still in place the brazier, together with the seating presented by M. Nigidius Vascula; and a *calidarium* of which the basin was installed in A.D. 3-4, by Cn. Melissius Aper and M. Statius Rufus.

The women's wing was similarly organized, except that the *frigidarium* was connected with the *apodyterium.* The furnace (*praefurnium*) lay between the two wings, the hot air circulating through a system of double walls (*concameratio*) and of paving raised on *suspensurae.* The rooms were elegantly decorated in painted stucco, with mythological scenes, foliate ornament and caryatid figures. A porticoed palestra occupied a part of the site.

THE HOUSE OF THE TRAGIC POET

A typical example of a Pompeian house with tuscan atrium and peristyle, and an upper storey, accessible from the atrium. It is richly and eleganted decorated with painting and mosaics. In the entrance is a pavement depicting a dog on a chain and the words *cave canem* ("beware of the dog").The wall-paintings of the atrium were large pictures of mytho-logical subjects, including Zeus and Hera, and Achilles and Briseis. Off the atrium opened the bedrooms and the *alae*, both well decorated, and in the centre of the rear wall the *tablinum*, in which were a small mosaic panel of theatrical actors and a picture of Admetus and Alcestis. A small portico occupies three sides of the peristyle. Here there was another well-known painting, the Sacrifice of Iphigenia, after Pheimantes (5th-4th century B.C.), and at the back a lararium.

The Forum Baths: calidarium

21

Off the portico open three rooms, one of them a dining room decorated in the Fourth Style with other mythological subjects (Venus and Cupids, Ariadne Abandoned, Diana). Some of the paintings and the mosaic panel are in the Naples Museum.

THE HOUSE OF SALLUST *(REG. VI)*

A typical example of a Pompeian house of the Samnite period, built in squared tufa masonry, with a Tuscan atrium; the doors are taller than they are wide and taper gently upward. To this period also belongs the well-preserved First Style wall-decoration. Various additions were made during the first century of the Empire - a little peristyle with hexagonal columns; a courtyard garden (*viridarium*), and a bakery (*pistrinum*). A typical sign of the times and of the changing needs of the owners is the opening of two shops on either side of the main entrance.

THE HERCULANEUM GATE

The ancient name of this was the *Porta Saliniensis* (Oscan "Veru Sarinu"), leading as it did to the village (*pagus* or *vicus*) of the *Salinienses*, whose inhabitants worked in the salt-pans. It also served the road to Herculaneum, whence the modern name. It stands at the end of the Via Consolare, and in its present form, with three arches, a broad opening in the centre for vehicles and two smaller ones for foot-passengers, it represents the form which it assumed during the Roman period, after it had lost all defensive function. For the city's defences in their various stages of development one must turn instead to the various traces of the fortifications of Pompei,

The Herculaneum Gate: reconstruction

of which the most ancient phases go back to the 6th century B.C. During the 5th century over the same line of the pre-existing wall, a lime-stone fortification was raised. The external curtain wall was built during the Samnite period (2nd century B.C.); the wall of concreted rubble masonry and the towers can be dated to the following century and are slightly earlier than the Social wars and the siege by the Romans.

THE STREET OF THE TOMBS (Via delle Tombe)

Outside the Herculaneum Gate lies the Street of the Tombs. Not yet completely excavated, it is one of the most suggestive corners of Pompeii, sloping gently down the hillside towards the plain and the sea and flanked on both sides, as was customary in the classical world, by funerary monuments, with here and there also the entries to suburban villas, and porticoes with shops. On the left-hand side the most interesting monuments are the "Tomb of the Garlands", of Republican date, so-called from the ornament of its architrave; and the "Tomb of the Blue Vase", from the vase of white-on-blue cameo-glass with cupids gathering grapes that was found in it and is now in the Naples museum. On the same side

The Street of the Tombs

lies the entrance to the " Villa of the Mosaic Columns", on the site of an earlier Samnite cemetery (3rd century B.C.); in the garden were found a large fountain faced with glass paste and shells and, similarly ornamented, the four columns of a pergola (now in the Naples Museum) after which it is named. Next, after a row of shops, the road forks. Beyond the fork, on the left, lies the "Villa of Diomede", followed by a group of monuments of noble citizens: of Umbricius Scaurus, with gladiatorial scenes in stucco; of Calventius Quietus; of Saturninus, in the form of a banqueting couch; of Munatius Faustus; and various funerary precincts, marble ornaments (notable among them that erected on the tomb of Munatius Faustus by his wife, Naevoleia Tyche, with representations of a funeral ceremony and a ship) and inscriptions; and finally the large and wealthy "Villa of Cicero", no longer visible because reburied soon after its discovery in 1763. Near the Herculaneum Gate there is another fine group of funerary monuments, among them that of the Istacidii family in the form of a temple on a podium, and that of the priestess Mamia, in the form of an exedra.

House of the Large Fountain:
the fountain with mosaic

25

THE HOUSE OF MELEAGER *(REG. VI)*

From the Via di Mercurio one enters into this house, which might be termed a luxury house, going back to the Samnite period but refurbished and redecorated in the 1st century A.D. with paintings and stuccoes in the fashionable Fourth Style. A large pool with marble ornaments occupies the centre of the graceful peristyle, and opening off the east portico a hall with a colonnade round the inner walls (a so-called *oecus corinthius*). A feature unusual for the period is the use of arches, instead of the familiar flat architrave, in this colonnade.

THE HOUSE OF THE LARGE FOUNTAIN *(REG. VI)*

This house takes its name from an unusual feature of its garden, namely a fountain in the shape of a niche faced with polychrome glass-paste mosaic, from which water pours into a basin.

Masks and statuettes add to the wealth of ornament. A feature worthy of note is the main door into the house, which is built of fine, squared tufa masonry, and opens onto via di Mercurio.

THE HOUSE OF THE FAUN *(REG. VI)*

The largest and finest house in Pompeii, remarkable alike for the dignity of its architecture, for the sober refinement of its First-Style wall-decoration, in squares of polished stucco imitating slabs of variegated marble, and for the high quality of its mosaics (now in the Naples Museum).

House of the Faun: reconstruction of the atrium

The pavement in front of the entrance bears the greeting, *have*; within it, high in the walls, are two lararia; and beyond it the Tuscan atrium, with a bronze statuette of a dancing Faun, a fine Hellenistic original of the 3rd-2nd century B.C., in the impluvium. Off the atrium open the bedrooms and, at the far end, the tablinum and two dining rooms, one for winter use with a mosaic of marine creatures, and one for autumn with Dionysus riding a panther. To the right of the atrium there is another living quarters with its own atrium of which the roof is supported on four columns (a "tetrastyle atrium"). Beyond lies the first peristyle, with porticoes on Ionic columns and a fountain in the middle of the garden and, opening off one side, the service rooms (kitchen, bath, etc.); at the far end two more dining rooms, for spring and summer use, and a large hall, the pavement of which portrayed the Battle of Alexander, a magnificent composition based on the work of one of the great Greek artists (now in Naples Museum), and in the entrance, a Nilotic scene. Beyond this again lies a second and much larger peristyle, with a two-storeyed Doric portico. The house had an upper storey, of which little is left. The House of the Faun was built in the 2nd century B.C., in the Samnite period, and shows how strong Hellenistic influence was on the Italic architecture of the time. As for the majority of the houses in Pompei, the name of the family who lived in this house is not known, however it must have been one of the main families of Pompei's Samnite period. Therefore the fact should be stressed that their house kept on to the end of the life of the city its original decorations (to which subtle allegorical meanings have been attributed), overcoming without apparent changes a period which certainly was of great turmoil to the life of Pompei, that is that of the social war and of the resulting settling as a Roman colony in the year 80 B.C.

THE HOUSE OF THE VETTII *(REG. VI)*

A luxurious house, the plan of which varies somewhat from the traditional model. Whereas the House of the Faun embodies the Greek artistic tastes and culture of the Samnite nobility, this house represents the last phase of wealthy private building by the well-to-do commercial classes. Its owners, Aulus Vettius Conviva and Aulus Vettius Restitutus, were merchants who undertook a radical restoration after the earthquake of 62. It is deservedly famous for the wealth of its Fourth Style decoration. Outside there are no *tabernae* or shops to strike a sordid commercial note. The entrance leads straight into a spacious atrium containing two strong-boxes (*arcae*); around the walls above the plinth runs a graceful frieze of cupids and spirits. Noteworthy among the several rooms opening off it is that on the left of the entrance, decorated with fantastic architecture, which frames small mythological pictures of Ariadne Abandoned and of Hero and Leander beneath a frieze of marine

creatures; and in the next room others of Cyparissus and the wounded stag and of Pan and Eros. There is no *tablinum*, but the peristyle is unusually elaborate and contains a garden that has been

House of the Vettii: the peristyle

29

House of the Vettii: frieze with Cupids as Goldsmiths

replanted with the same plants as in antiquity, forming a most attractive and suggestive setting for the fountains and sculpture that were found in it.

Three rooms open off the portico. The first is decorated with false architectural perspectives, seascape panels and pictures of figured subjects - Daedalus and Pasiphae, Ixion bound to his wheel, and Dionysus and Ariadne; the second with a similar setting and pictures of Hercules strangling the snakes, the Punishment of Pentheus and the Punishment of Dirce. The third is the great dining room, one of the most elegant decorative schemes yet found in the private houses of Pompeii. The field is red, divided by black panels simulating the arches of a loggia and decorated with Menads and satyrs. Below it runs a frieze of the most delicate, spirited workmanship, portraying cupids engaged in such varied occupations as selling oil, chariot-racing, goldsmith's work, the vintage, selling wine, etc. The plinth too is subdivided, floral ornaments alternating with figured panels with Psyches, mythical scenes and pairs of lovers. The service rooms are grouped round a secondary *atrium* with an upper storey, and beyond this again lie the women's quarters (*gynaeceum*).

THE HOUSE OF THE GOLDEN CUPIDS (*REG. VI*)

The architectural plan of this house goes back to the Republican age, while the interior decoration can be dated to the Imperial era, around the mid of the 1st century A.D. The Tuscan atrium is simply planned, with a bed-chamber on either side of the entrance and a *tablinum* at the far end; from the atrium and the tablinum doors lead into the peristyle beyond. The latter is displaced towards the left, and around it runs a handsome Doric portico with a garden in the centre and a variety of marble decorative sculpture - carved panels, *oscilla*, herms and theatrical masks. The living quarters lie along the wings of the portico, of which the

House of the Vettii:Hercules strangling the snakes

31

west side is raised on several steps, like a stage-building with three doors and a crowning pediment. These arrangements suggest that the owner was interested in the theatre, and he seems also to have been interested in the cult of the Egyptian goddess Isis, of whom there is a shrine in the north portico. The name of the house derives from the small glass discs to be seen in the bed-chamber, framing figures of Cupids delicately incised on gold foil.

THE HOUSE OF L. CAECILIUS JUCUNDUS *(REG. V)*

The residence of one L. Caecilius Jucundus, who exercised the profession of a banker, at any rate until the year of the earthquake. In it were found the well-preserved and still legible business records of Jucundus, full of information about the economic life of the time and in particular about the financial operations of Jucundus himself. In the atrium were found a portrait herm of the banker's father, L. Caecilius Felix, one of the finest pieces recovered from the soil of Pompeii, and a *lararium* with two very interesting marble reliefs, naif but most expressive portrayals of a group of Pompeian buildings at the moment of the earthquake: on the one side the Forum, with the Temple of Jupiter and one of the honorary arches, and on the other the Vesuvius Gate, the walls and the *castellum aquae* which regulated the water supply. They are certainly ex-voto offerings (perhaps for the escape of Caecilius), and for all their failings as works of art they offer a vivid glimpse of the results of the earthquake.

THE HOUSE OF THE SILVER WEDDING (REG. V)

This house, one of the most luxurious in Pompeii, takes its name from the fact of its excavation in 1893, the year of the silver wedding of Umberto and Margherita di Savoia. Its last owner was a rich and influential citizen, L. Albucius Celsus. Built in the Samnite period, it underwent various alterations during the 1st century A.D. The noble atrium, with four tall columns supporting the roof, is decorated in the Second Style. The peristyle, a later addition, is of the type called Rhodian, in which one of the porticoes is taller than the others; its columns were subsequently faced in stucco, the lower parts smooth and the upper parts hexagonal. The decoration of the walls is of the Fourth Style. Adjoining it is a garden with an open-air *triclinium*. The elegant living rooms round the peristyle include one, which may have been a *triclinium*, of which the vault is carried on four

House of The Centenary: painting of Bacchus and Vesuvius

columns (*oecus corinthius*) imitating red porphyry and the walls are decorated in the Second Style. There is also a large room with black walls, an exedra with a yellow bakground and a small bathing-suite.

There was an upper storey to the rooms round the atrium.

THE HOUSE OF THE CENTENARY *(REG. IX)*

A very large house with two atria, the property of Aulus Rustius Verus, excavated in 1879 on the occasion of the eighteenth century from the burial of Pompei. The first atrium has a mosaic floor and is decorated in the Fourth Style with small panels of theatrical subjects; beyond it lie the *tablinum* and a peristyle, the front wing of which forms a loggia.

In the garden was found the celebrated statuette of a satyr with a wine-skin; also a small mosaic-ornamented fountain. In the *lararium* of the second, smaller atrium was found the well-known painting of Bacchus and Vesuvius (now in the National Museum in Naples); it leads to a group of rooms finely decorated with mythological scenes and to a bath.

THE CENTRAL BATHS *(REG. IX)*

These occupy an entire block, at the junction of the Via di Nola and the Via di Stabia; built in brick, with much reuse of earlier materials, they were begun after the earthquake and were still unfinished when buried by the eruption. They represent a new, more strictly functional architectural scheme for this type of building, characterised by a more spacious and internally coherent lay-out, and by the use of windows for light and air, and of a single bathing-circuit, not divided into separate wings for men and women.

The main entrance is from the Via di Nola, leading into the palaestra court-yard, along the east side of which lie the bath-buildings proper; a changing-room (*apodyterium*) with a circular cold plunge, the *tepidarium*, and a *calidarium* with large niches in the walls of the long sides. A feature new to the traditional scheme is the *laconicum*, a circular room for the *sudatio*.

House of the Silver Wedding: the atrium

35

Descending the Via di Stabia and taking the first turn to the right (Reg. VII) one arrives at the *Pistrinum*.

PISTRINUM (Bakery) *(REG. VII)*

The burial of Pompeii took place very rapidly. The inhabitants were barely able to escape carrying a few personal belongings; indeed, many failed to get away at all and died, victims of their own hesitation and of the poisonous fumes. The rain of ash and cinders was not, on the other hand, unduly destructive, and it preserved much of what it buried. The result has been to make Pompeii a dead city as fascinating to the visitor as it is instructive to the student of antiquity. Monuments and work of art are to be found on many archaeological sites; here we can see also the little things of daily life, almost perfectly preserved, and study the tangible traces of habits and customs that are recorded nowhere else, often not even in the classical texts. Examples of this are the shops, with their counters and containers for food stuffs and other goods; the workshops with their tools, the furniture still standing in place within the houses; and the inscriptions on the walls, which plunge us straight into the middle of a municipal electoral campaign.

This shows us all the essential elements of a *pistrinum* for making bread. In the middle are the mills. These are made of smooth basalt from Vesuvius or one of the other volcanic areas of Campania, and consist of a conical stone (*meta*) standing on circular masonry basis and, resting and rotating on the *meta*, a second, biconical stone hollowed out internally (*catillus*). A wooden framework with two horizontal arms allowed the latter to be turned either by human or by animal

The Bakery: reconstruction

power, as one can understand from a painting in another bakery of the same region where a donkey, frequently used for this function, is shown behind Vesta on her Throne. The grain was poured into the upper hollow of the *catillus* and came out at the bottom ground into flour.

On the right are a series of long, low supports for the tables for preparing and stacking the loaves, and on the left was the oven for baking them. Next to the bakery was the shop. Many carbonized loaves have been found here and there in the excavations, giving us a good idea of the appearance of what was then, as now, the staple item of diet. A scratched inscription refers to the excellence of the Pompeian bread.

THE STABIAN BATHS (*REG. VII*)

These, the oldest public baths in Pompeii, take their name from their situation on the crossing of the Via Stabiana and the Via dell'Abbondanza. One can distinguish at least five building periods. Built in the Samnite period (2nd century B.C.), they were first restored and enlarged in the early years of the Roman colony, then again under the Empire, and finally once more after the earthquake. These last repairs were still unfinished, and the baths still out of action, at the moment of the eruption.

The Stabian Baths are an outstanding example of a type of building which was very common in the Roman world, and which with the centuries underwent many changes of structure and function.

The principal entrance, on the Via dell'Abbondanza, leads through a small, square vestibule into the palaestra, which was surrounded by porticoes on three sides. In the last restoration the

The Stabian Baths: reconstruction

pool and a series of changing-rooms. Here the athletes anointed themselves with oil and sand before exercising, afterwards scraping off the sweat and dust with a strigil.

VIA DELL'ABBONDANZA

The stretch of the lower decumanus that runs from the Forum to the Sarno Gate takes the name of Via dell'Abbondanza from a relief which adorns a public fountain near the Forum end and which has been thought to represent the goddess of Abundance. It was probably the principal artery of the city, like the other *decumanus,* the Via di Nola, running the whole length of it and connecting all the principal centres: the Forum, the Stabian Baths, the Theatre quarter and the temple of Isis, and finally the Amphitheatre and the great Palaestra. It is also the part of the excavations which comes to life most readily for the visitor, thanks to the up-to-date methods of its excavation and conservation. Greater attention to the surviving superstructures and a better technique of restoration have made possible the recomposition and consolidation of whatever came from the upper storeys.

The result has been to acquire much new and often quite unexpected knowledge about this particular aspect of ancient architecture (upper storeys with terraces and small porticoes, often bracketed out from the facade below) and in many respects also to change traditional beliefs about the Roman atrium house. Another innovation has been to leave all objects where they were found, so that one can now see in place, painted in large red letters on the stucco of the house facades, the electoral posters, and beside them innumerable smaller painted or scratched texts, verses and poems, imprecations, lampoons and obscenities. The main shops hang out their signs to attract customers, and laid out on the counters and shelves are glasses, terracottas and bronzes. The workshops of the artisans contain the tools and equipment of their craft, and from the surviving decoration of the houses and the objects in use we can form an impression of the varying social status of the houses - a variety far greater than one would ever have imagined. The large *House of the Cryptoporticus* is remarkable for its elaborate plan and for the covered gallery which gives it its name, finely decorated in the Second Style and converted into a cellar by its last owner. The nearby *House of Paquius Proculus* on the other hand has preserved its handsome atrium with a figured mosaic pavement and its spacious peristyle. Across the street the *House of the Moralist,* with its painted epigrams in the dining-room, offers a glimpse of Pompeian society behaviour, while the *Thermopolium* (Bar) *delle Aselline* embodies the less polished manners of the tavern world. As one moves away from the centre towards the *Porta di Sarno* the houses grow less and less urban in character, both in lay-out and in the proportion of open space, approximating increasingly to the suburban villas. Past the *House of the Venus*, the *House of Octavius Quartio* and the *Villa of Julia Felix*, one passes in almost logical sequence out into the open countryside beyond the walls, out into the ever-fertile *Ager Pompeianus*.

Via dell'Abbondanza: reconstruction

THE HOUSE OF D. OCTAVIUS QUARTIO (*REG. II*)

The door with its great bronze nails is based on a plaster cast; the atrium is plain and the impluvium has become a flower bed. The best part of the house is the peristyle and the annexed pergola-covered loggia; the paintings of Pyramus and Thisbe and of Narcissus in the triclinium at the far end, though unpretentious, are unusual because at the time of their excavation the signature of the *Lucius pinxit* could be read. On the wall of one large hall are two bands of fine painted scenes from the story of Hercules and the Trojan cycle, and included among the elegant Fourth Style paintings of a small room opening off the west side of it is a figure of a priest of Isis, which is perhaps a portrait of one of the house's occupants.

Below the loggia, in the large garden (*hortus*) beyond, runs a small channel (*euripus*) with miniature cascades, a tank with a fountain and a tempietto; along the edge are ornamental statuettes, animals, muses, marble herms, and along on either side of it ran paths shaded by pergolas. All of these elements are typical of the great villas, of which this 'little villa in the city' offers a miniature reproduction.

THE HOUSE OF THE VENUS (*REG. II*)

This is another of the Pompeian houses which at the time of the eruption had not yet completely recovered from the earthquake. This is particularly clear in the mosaic-paved dining-room, of which the walls are merely plastered in readiness for the customary painted decoration.

The main rooms are disposed along the wings of the garden. On two sides of this are porticoes, the columns stuccoed and painted in golden yellow and white, while the rear wall is painted with a scheme that reflects its setting, depicting a hedge with flowering shrubs, marble basins with doves drinking from them and a statue of Mars on a base. The subject of the central scene is quite different, representing Venus skimming the ocean, reclining in a cockle-shell with two attendant cupids. The merits of the picture lie in its lively colour and decorative qualities rather than its artistry, and it offers a vivid illustration of the capacities and limitations of the local artists in interpreting and reelaborating the familiar mythological subjects which they inherited from other and abler hands.

House of the Venus: painting of a statue of Mars

45

THE VILLA OF JULIA FELIX *(REG. II)*

This is a large residence, laid out on an unusual plan. A door from the Via dell'Abbondanza, painted with scenes showing life in the Forum, leads through a large vestibule into the portico around the garden. This has slender, elegant marble pilasters and off it open a series of rooms, notably a triclinium with marble-façade couches and in the rear wall an aedicula, which emitted a cascade of water into a channel beneath. In the south side there is a shrine, perhaps for the cult of Isis.

At the far end are the living quarters, with service rooms round an atrium and an entrance from the alley to the west. The garden forms an elongated rectangle, with pilasters, probably for a pergola, on the other two sides and a fish-pool down the centre, with miniature bridges and marble niches. A separate entrance from the Via dell'Abbondanza leads to the *balneum*. This is a small, well designed bath-building which, as we learn from an inscription (which gives the owner's name) was built and rented out for public use. It includes a small porticoed courtyard, a changing-room with a cold plunge, a *tepidarium*, a *calidarium* and a circular *laconicum* for *sudationes* (dry sweating); also an open air pool, furnace and latrine. Alongside the villa is a large orchard, and fronting on to the street a tavern and row of two-storeyed shops, which must also have been rented out.

The Villa, excavated and reburied in the mid-18th century, was again uncovered in 1952-53. Some of the rich decoration in marble, painting and sculpture was dispersed by the original excavators (some paintings showing Apollo and the Muses are now in the Louvre, and others are in Naples Museum), but finds in the recent excavation included a terracotta statuette of Pittacus of Mytilene.

The Villa of Julia Felix: reconstruction

THE AMPHITHEATRE

The oldest known Roman amphitheatre. It was erected about 80 B.C. under the duoviri C. Quintius Valgus and M. Porcius, who also built the Little Theatre.

The arena is at a lower level than the surrounding ground, so that the building is partly sunk and lacks substructures. The seats were reached by external staircases. There are substantial remains of the seating, as well as of the upper gallery, reserved for women. Inside the building was decorated with paintings representing the various games that took place in the amphitheatre. It constitutes a valuable document for the early development of a type of monument which was very popular in Roman times, and which was subsequently developed and elaborated in the great amphitheatres of the Imperial age.

The seating was shaded by a *velarium* (canopy) supported by poles, as we learn from the programmes of the games and as can be seen in the famous painting (kept in the Naples Museum) showing the riot that exploded between the inhabitants of Pompeii and Nuceria in the year 59 A.D.

The restorations undertaken after the earthquake were probably the work of the duoviri C. Cuspius Pansa and his son.

THE PALAESTRA

Alongside is a huge palaestra, with an enclosing wall and porticoes on three sides. The swimming pool in the centre was surrounded by a double row of plane-trees.

The amphitheatre

THE HOUSE OF THE MENANDER *(REG. I)*

Like the House of the Golden Cupids this belonged to a branch of the influential family of the *Poppaei*. The entrance is flanked by two dignified pilasters with Corinthian capitals. Within the Tuscan atrium, decorated in the Fourth Style, is the Lararium and in one of the rooms opening

off it a series of small panels depicting episodes from the Trojan cycle: Laocoon, the Trojan Horse, Cassandra. Beyond the *tablinum* lie the fine columnar peristyle and a series of rooms, one of which has an elegant decorative scheme on a green background with cupids among vineshoots and a mosaic pavement containing a Nilotic panel; another, a large dining-room, incorporates at a lower level earlier structures decorated in the Second Style. An *exedra* at the back has paintings showing in the center Diana inside a small temple. Another *exedra* has theatrical paintings including a portrait of the poet Menander, whence the name of the house. Along one side lies the bath-suite, elegantly decorated with paintings and mosaics; off the other lie the domestic quarters. In the basement was found a silver service of 115 pieces, now in the Naples Museum.

House of the Menander: portrait of the poet

THE TEMPLE OF ISIS *(REG. VIII)*

The sanctuary of an Egyptian cult that attained great popularity in the Roman world, it was first built during the IInd century B.C. and was completely rebuilt after the earthquake of 62 through the generosity of Numerius Popidius Celsinus. It is the most complete of the city's temples. Building, decoration and sacred furnishings were all perfectly preserved, when found (1764-1766). Paintings and sculptures are now in a room of Naples Museum which reconstructs and respects as much as possible the original aspect of the decoration. The precinct is surrounded by a high wall, with a single entrance so situated that from the street nothing could be seen of the ceremonies conducted within the enclosure. The small temple stands on a tall podium and consists of a porch and a cella, within which were the sacred objects characteristic of the Isiac cult. Below, near the steps, is the altar; at the south-east corner of the court there is a roofless enclosure from where one descended into an underground cavity in which was kept the sacred Nile water; and on the other side a covered enclosure served as a repository for the ashes and remains of sacrifices. Behind the temple there is a large hall which was built on an area which originally belonged to the neighbouring Samnite palaestra.

THE TRIANGULAR FORUM *(REG. VIII)*

The Triangular Forum, which took its shape from the stretch of level ground in which it was built, is another centre that was linked with buildings of a public character; it was entered through a vestibule with ionic columns and flanked internally by two Doric porticoes, raised during the

Samnite period and which mark the importance of the area in the middle of which stood a Doric temple of the mid 6th century B.C. thought to associate the cult of Athena with that of Hercules. Partly destroyed in the Samnite period, only the basis and scanty fragments of the superstructure survive, including architectural terracottas. In Roman times it was reduced to a mere shrine. Other features of the Forum were a statue of Marcellus, August's nephew, three Samnite-period tufa altars, a circular aedicula with a well, and a semicircular seat (*exedra*) with a sundial.

From the east portico of the forum a door gave access to a palaestra also built in the Samnite period, in which was found a copy of the Doryphoros of Polycleitos; and another door led to the *summa cavea* of the Large Theatre. There was access also, by means of a broad flight of steps, to the spacious portico enclosure which lies behind the stage-building of the theatre.

THE THEATRE *(REG. VIII)*

Pompeii had two theatres, a smaller, roofed Odeon for recitations, musical performances and mimes, and a larger theatre which was open but could if necessary be covered with an awning. In its present form the latter dates from a restoration of the 1st century A.D.

The upper zone of seating (*summa cavea*) is raised on a vaulted corridor (*crypta*), the middle and lower zones rest on the ground, with the *tribunalia* for distinguished spectators set over the entrances to the orchestra. It held about 5000 spectators. The orchestra, no longer used by actors and chorus, was also available for seating, probably for citizens of the upper classes. There was a low stage of Roman type, the rear wall of which was carried up in an elaborate scheme of recesses and aediculae, with three doors to simulate the façade of a palace. Behind it lay a room

The Theatre: reconstruction

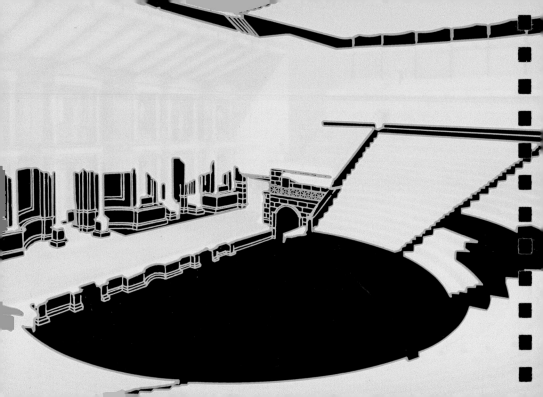

used by the actors, and beyond this again a rectangular space enclosed by porticoes. This was the *porticus post scaenam* used by the spectators in the intervals or in bad weather. The name of the architect of the theatre in this, its latest, form is known - M. Artorius Primus, a contemporary of Augustus.

There had been earlier structural phases. The original building, was built in the IInd century B.C. within the context of the urban development of this part of the city, following a Hellenistic model, had limestone tiers which followed for the greater part the natural slope of the hillside and was smaller than the present one. Some structural alterations can be dated towards the beginning of the 1st century B.C., whereas the enlarging of the *cavea*, the seating for the spectators, can be attributed to the period of Augustus and was obtained with the construction of an elevated upper zone, *summa cavea*, over the crypt and held up by the arches and pilasters, and the marble covering of the steps, and the remodelling of the *tribunalia*. The *frons scaenae* (the "back-cloth") maybe could be of a period subsequent to the earthquake of 62 A.D. For the work of M. Artorius Primus, mentioned above, and for the munificence of the two distinguished citizens, M. Holconius Rufus and M. Holconius Celer, who paid for it, we have a group of inscriptions found in the theatre.

The *velarium* (awning) that gave shade to the building, was held up by pilasters which were inserted in the *summa cavea* and was stretched and adjusted as required by means of a system of ropes and pulleys. The *velarium* that covered the *frons scaenae* worked in a similar way.

THE ODEON *(REG. VIII)*

The Small Theatre, or Odeon, held about 1000 spectators and was intended for more intimate programmes such as concerts, recitations of verses and mimes. It was built about the year 80 B.C. by the duoviri C. Quintius Valgus and M. Porcius. Unlike the Large Theatre it had a permanent timber roof, probably with four slopes. There are only two zones of seating, the upper one of which was separated from the lower by a balustrade and the seats are almost completely preserved; a pair of *telamon* figures carved in tufa mark the ends of the parapets on either side.

The paving of the orchestra, furnished by the duovir M. Oculatius Verus, was of marble, as must also have been the facing of the stage.

The remodelling of the balustrade and the construction of the *tribunalia* can probably be ascribed to a modification carried out during the period of Augustus. For the rest the building maintained the original balance of its plan, structure and ornament. The result is an unusually harmonious example of late Hellenistic taste and one which constitutes an important landmark in the architectural history of Pompeii.

THE SUBURBAN VILLAS

THE VILLA OF THE MYSTERIES

The finest example of a suburban villa, renowned alike for its size and its many wall-paintings, notably those of the dining-room from which the villa takes its name. Not yet completely cleared, it stands a short distance outside the town beyond the Herculaneum Gate and was entered

from a street which presumably connected with the Via delle Tombe. Between the entrance and the peristyle lies the domestic wing with a kitchen, a bakery with its oven, the *prelum* for pressing the grapes, the wine cellar and the slaves' quarters. The domestic wing (through which one now enters) is disposed about a *tablinum* and *atrium*, with a wall decoration reproducing marble-slabs, which opens off the peristyle, also decorated in the same way. The nucleus of the villa goes back to the 2nd century B.C., but it later under-

The Villa of the Mysteries: the atrium

went several enlargements and restorations, enjoying a period of brilliance as a patrician villa and then as Imperial property. In its last years it passed to the family of the Istacidii who converted it into a villa rustica. The great frieze that occupies the walls of the dining-room is the work of a

Campanian artist of the 1st century B.C. under the influence of Greek painting. There is considerable dispute among scholars about the exact significance of these paintings, but there seems to be no doubt that they are in some way related to the mystery cults, and they are usually thought to represent the successive stages of a bride's initiation into the mysteries of Dionysus.

Starting with the north wall and reading from left to right, the cycle begins with a child, guided by a seated matron, reading from a papyrus the regulations for the sacred rites. There follows a scene of offerings and sacrifice, and a pastoral scene with a Silen playing the lyre; and at the end of the wall, a woman starting back in terror. In the middle of east wall the marriage of Dionysus and Ariadne symbolises the happiness that awaits the initiated in the after-world; on the left a Silen and two Satyrs, and on the right a woman unveiling the symbol of fertility and a winged figure raising a scourge. Next comes a woman being scourged, who hides her face

The Villa of the Mysteries,
Fresco of the fleeing girl

57

in the lap of a companion, followed by a nude, dancing Bacchante. To complete the cycle there are two portraits of the matron, one completing her toilet, the other seated and mantled, already initiated and the mystic bride of the god. Both in content and in quality these paintings are among the finest preserved from antiquity.

Neighbouring the dining-room there is a cubicle with two alcoves with red background decorations, of which also the upper part is well conserved.

THE VILLA OF DIOMEDE

The discovery of this villa in 1771-74 made a great impression on the archaeological and literary world, not least because of the finding of eighteen bodies in the underground portico. Unfortunately, except for some paintings in Naples Museum, little survives on the spot of the rich decoration which marked it out as an upper-class residence. After the Villa of the Mysteries it is the most important suburban building yet excavated.

A discrete but tasteful entrance, set within a small portico, leads from the Via delle Tombe into the Peristyle. A triangular area on the east side houses the baths, with a small portico and a pool for bathing. The dwelling rooms lie to the north and south and include a room with three windows and an apse, preceded by an anteroom. From the same side one passes through the *tablinum*, which was later enlarged by the construction of a large room built partly over the portico beneath; thence to other rooms and to a second terrace which runs right round the garden, serving as an *ambulatio* and *solarium*, for exercise and sunshine. A ramp and staircase led down to the spacious square garden, in the middle of which were a large pool and a summer dining-room

surrounded by columns.Round it ran a portico with windows (later closed) facing outwards and two belvedere turrets at the angles of the side towards the sea. Two small flights of steps led down into the cryptoportico, lit by small splay-windows facing inwards and outwards; it was also used as a cellar. The position is a fine one, and the villa was obviously laid out so that both the terrace and the dwelling rooms should make the best use both of the view and of the sunshine.

THE ANTIQUARIUM

This offers a broad documentation of the history and art of Pompeii through a display of typical finds. In the entrance, wall-maps illustrating the progress of the excavations from 1748 to 1948.

In Room I, the protohistory of the Sarno Valley (9th-8th century B.C.); architectural terracottas from the Doric Temple and the Temple of Apollo (6th-5th century B.C.); fragments of Greek pottery and archaic Etruscan bucchero. In Room II, sculpture of the Samnite period (3rd-2nd century B.C.); the sphinx from the fondo Barbatelli, composite capitals with figures of Maenads and Satyrs; metope with the punishment of Ixion; pediment of the Dionysiac shrine outside the city, with Dionysus and Ariadne. In the next room, Roman portraits: Livia, wife of Augustus, and Marcellus, his nephew; Cornelius Rufus, Vesonius Primus, Suedius Clemens and other Pompeian worthies. Finally, two rooms in which are displayed remains illustrating the daily life of Pompeii: bronze furniture, jewellery, wall-paintings, small decorative sculpture of the Roman period; also plaster casts of bodies and of other objects, and a small-scale model of the Boscoreale villa rustica.

HERCULANEUM
INTRODUCTION AND HISTORICAL SUMMARY

Herculaneum was a small township on the slopes of Vesuvius, near the sea and not far from the Greek colony of *Neapolis*. Myth attributed its foundation to Hercules, and it is likely enough that it was founded very early. For a while it came under the political and cultural influence of Cuma and *Neapolis*, before falling to the Samnite invaders of Campania at the end of the 5th century B.C. It was probably involved in the Samnite wars, and later it took part in the Social War, when it revolted against Rome, was subdued by Titus Didius, Sulla's legate, in 89 B.C., and was turned into a Roman *municipium*. Like Pompeii Herculaneum was badly damaged in the earthquake of 62, and in 79 fell victim to the eruption; but instead of being buried in a rain of ash and cinders, it was overwhelmed by clouds of scorching toxic gas,alternated at least six times with torrents of volcanic mud,which swept away persons,objects and structures, even uprooting the roofs of the houses and which ,in gradually burying the city, covered it entirely and solidified into a compact shelf of rock, like tufa in appearance and consistency. On this occasion the ground level rose by an average of some 50 feet. The same flows, in reaching the sea, determined the advancing of the coast line for about 1,000 feet and a seaquake as well. After the eruption, emperor

HERCULANEUM

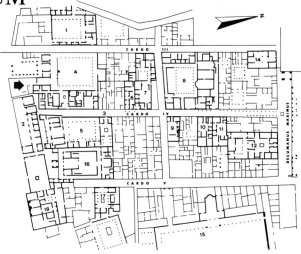

1 The House of Argo
2 Sacred Precinct and Terraced
   Houses
3 Cardo IV
4 The House of the Inn
5 The House of the Mosaic
   Atrium
6 The House of the Latticework
7 The House of the Wooden
   Screen
8 The Forum Baths
9 The Samnite House
10 The House of the Carbonized
   Furniture
11 The House of Poseidon and
   Amphitrite
12 The House of the Bicentenary
13 The Decumanus Maximus
14 The Basilica
15 The Palaestra
16 The House of the Stags
17 The House of the Telephus
   Relief
18 The Suburban Baths

62

Titus sent two commissioners on the spot to assign the property of those victims without heirs to indemnify the stricken surviving citizens. Nevertheless according to ancient sources and findings from excavations, the site was, at least partially, reoccupied afterwards in Antiquity.

The rediscovery of Herculaneum was accidental. In 1711 the Prince of Elbeuf, commander of the Austrian fleet, ordered a well to be a dug in a property of his in the wood of the Frati Alcantarini and in digging it came upon the ruins of the theatre. From it came marbles and sculpture, which were then dispersed, some of them to the Museum of Dresden. The systematic excavation of the city began only in 1738 on the orders of King Charles of Bourbon, who later founded the Academy of Herculaneum for the study and publication of the finds.

The circumstances of the city's burial practically precluded an open excavation, and in consequence the early exploration of Herculaneum was undertaken by means of shafts and horizontal underground galleries, the skilled excavators following the courses of streets and houses to bring to light pictures, mosaics, sculptures and other objects which went to form the Herculaneum Museum, housed in the nearby palace of Portici. The remarkable quality of the finds was at once apparent, in some respects even better than those of Pompeii. Exploration continued to be conducted by means of shafts and galleries until 1765; but when, after a long interval, it was resumed in 1828 the system adopted was that of open digging. Excavation is still in progress, but it is a very slow business, partly because of the practical difficulties of freeing the remains from their casing of rock and of diverting the waters that tend to accumulate in the lowest quarters as a result of a rise in the sea-level, partly because the site lies beneath the town of Resina and every extension involves the demolition of the houses above. A local Museum for the conservation of the recent finds has been opened in 1977.

The plan of Herculaneum, so far as it is known from the excavations and from the record of the Bourbon excavators, is extremely regular, with a rectangular, chess-board lay-out as in the neighbouring Graeco-Roman *Neapolis*. At the centre lay the Forum and the large public buildings around it. In the last phase of its history the city spread beyond its walls, towards the sea, and there were suburban villas in the surrounding countryside. One of these, the residence of the wealthy and cultivated Pisones, was explored between 1750 and 1765, yielding a rich haul of sculpture and a library of papyri. In 1986 its exploration was resumed by following the original galleries of the Bourbons in order to complete the excavation and to recover the rest of the library.

As far as one can tell in the present state of the excavations, Herculaneum was somewhat different in character from Pompeii. For one thing it was smaller, and in its manners and building-practices it kept more closely to the traditions inherited from the Samnite period. Its main activities were agriculture and fishing, in which the lower classes mingled freely with the representatives of families of ancient lineage; Seneca refers to a villa of Caligula, and Agrippina's mother was for a time banished here.

THE HOUSE OF ARGO

Excavated only in part at the beginning of the last century, the House of Argo appears to be one of the large terraced residences of the southern part of Herculaneum, and the equal of any of those described in the next sections. One enters today by what must have been a back entrance opening off *cardo* III; but even this is of some pretentions, with a porch projecting over the pavement. Within lies a large peristyle garden, with porticoes on three sides which give access

to a series of rooms, including a dining-room in the north wing. There was a second storey with bedrooms and food-stores, and a long balcony projecting over the street. Beyond lay a second peristyle, of which only a corner has been cleared; it too was evidently of grandiose proportions. The *atrium* quarter presumably lay on this side and still awaits discovery. The interesting underground chambers include a shrine for the household cult.

SACRED PRECINCT AND TERRACED HOUSES

At Herculaneum, as at Pompeii, there was a moment in the 1st century A.D. when, with the establishment of the Augustan peace, the city walls ceased to have any defensive purpose. Not only could the city expand beyond the walls, but the walls themseves began to be invaded by houses, serving as a nucleus for the new buildings, as in the case of the House of Aristides at the south western end. In this building a ramp paved with river stones has been uncovered which must have led to the sea-shore through a door in the walls corresponding to the entrance to the *cardo* III. The House of the Inn, the House of the Mosaic *Atrium* and the House of the Stags are examples

House of Argo: painting with sacellum

of such development at the south-west edge of the city. Without sacrificing the advantages of city life, the owners could enjoy the speading peristyle and gardens of a suburban villa, and by using the natural lie of the ground, they were able to reate dwelling-rooms and terraces with delightful views out towards the nearby sea. According to the most recent investigations the latter, before the eruption, reached-up to the southern front of the city where there was a small port: in this area in fact, a boat for transporting passengers has been found, which is now kept in the Museum, and which was obviously thrown onto the beach by the seaquake.

Outside the walls two important groups of buildings have been cleared, the baths and the sacred precinct. Here, however, to the already considerable difficulties of excavation in Herculaneum is added that created by the sinking of the land in relation to the sea, with the result that the ancient surface is at least 5 feet below present sea level, and that the monuments themselves are subject to continual seepage.

The sacred precinct is full of interest. From the entrance, opposite that of the enclosure of the Suburban Baths, a long corridor leads to the first shrine. On one side are a series of vaulted rooms, including the porter's lodge, the service rooms for the cult (in which were found two female statues) and a room with a hearth. The wall on the other side is pierced by doors and arches facing on to an open space which must have been maintained as a garden, with two marble basins. The shrine, which stands on a low platform, now consists only of a *cella* but must once have had a columnar porch; of its decoration the mosaic pavement and a fragment of wall-painting survive, and against the rear wall there is a plinth, with a marble table in front. The second shrine resembles the first but is larger, with a porch carried on four columns and a similar plinth, on which are the bases of two cult statues. Adjoining rooms presumably served the purposes of the cult. The names

Sacred Precinct and Terraced Houses: reconstruction

of the divinities worshipped are not known for certain, but they may have been Venus and Liber. The whole group of buildings was probably the seat of a religious association in charge of one of the public cults.

CARDO IV

The streets of Herculaneum which run downhill from north to south (*cardines*), following the natural slope, are paved with lava slabs between high sidewalks. Unlike Pompeii, there are no stepping stones for pedestrians to cross, and wheel ruts are few. What with the slope and the absence of mercantile and commercial interests, there were evidently few vehicles, pedestrians and animals accounting for most of the traffic. *Cardo* IV and the houses along it will serve to present a typical picture of life in this little Vesuvian city. Entering by the city-gate from the lowest levels of the suburban quarter, the first stretch of it runs for some distance between two large terraced houses, that of the Inn and that of the Mosaic *Atrium*, both of which are entered from it. There follow several fine, but smaller, houses of Samnite date (the House of the Bronze Herm, the House of the Wooden Screen, the Samnite House) interspersed with modest dwellings such as the House of the Latticework. After crossing the lower *decumanus*, the cardo on one side ran past the baths (with a door into the women's section) and the House of the Black Room, and on the other past a group of small but elegant houses such as that with the mosaic of Poseidon and Amphitrite. Beyond lies the crossing with the main *decumanus*. Here one can guess at the gathering tempo of urban life. This long, narrow street of ancient Herculaneum, with its porches

Cardo IV: reconstruction

and Amphitrite. Beyond lies the crossing with the main *decumanus*. Here one can guess at the gathering tempo of urban life. This long, narrow street of ancient Herculaneum, with its porches in front of the individual houses, its upper storeys, some of them projecting over the street, and the lively colours of its plaster renderings, must indeed have been a picturesque sight.

THE HOUSE OF THE INN (Casa dell'Albergo)

The traditional name is misleading. Like its neighbour, it was originally a wealthy patrician residence, which was later converted to mercantile and utilitarian uses. Most of the rooms lie round the *atrium*, and there is a bathing-block; beyond lies a huge orchard-garden and beside it a peristyle with reception rooms and a large terrace.

THE HOUSE OF THE MOSAIC ATRIUM

The entrance and the *atrium* are mosaic-paved, the latter with a chequer-board of black and white, which has sagged badly beneath the weight of the engulfing mud.

The *tablinum* is divided by pilasters into three naves, of which the central one is taller and lit by clerestory windows, a rare instance of a basilical *oecus aegyptius*.

Alongside lies a garden enclosed within a windowed portico with dwelling-rooms opening off it; and beyond this a large and luxurious dining-room and adjoining rooms which face out on to a covered loggia and to a terrace overlooking the view.

THE HOUSE OF THE LATTICEWORK (Casa a graticcio)

Built throughout in *opus craticium*, a poor type of construction which is found in other buildings at Herculaneum and Pompeii, but only in secondary structures. It consists of a framework of wood or a latticework of cane supporting panels of rubble masonry. The rooms are grouped in two storeys about a small courtyard and were divided into several small apartments. A porch in front of the building carries a small projecting loggia. There is a door leading into the cortile and another which serves a small apartment in the upper storey; and the shop connects with other ground-floor rooms for the use of some artisan.

THE HOUSE OF THE WOODEN SCREEN

A patrician residence which retains much of its original Samnite-period appearance despite modifications in the mid-1st century A.D., when it was enlarged behind so as to take in the whole block and upwards to include a second storey, and when the whole north wing was turned into shops.

House of the Mosaic Atrium: painted alcove

Around the large and well-proportioned *atrium*, decorated to the full height of the first storey were grouped the usual rooms: the bedrooms (*cubicula*), one of them with a geometrical mosaic pavement, the dining-room (*triclinum*) with Fourth Style paintings, and a living-room (*tablinum*) which is unique in having preserved the impression of the wooden screen that separated it from the *atrium*. This screen had double doors at either end, and in the middle, which is not preserved, what was probably a large, plain partition. The *tablinum* leads into a garden surrounded by a small pilastered portico with a loggia above, beyond which lie other living rooms and a dining-room. From the domestic nucleus one passes to the shops, which face on to the lower decumanus and on to *cardo* III.

THE FORUM BATHS

Herculaneum has so far yielded two large public bath-buildings. One of these is not far from the city centre and may be called the Forum Baths; the other lies outside the city

House of the Wooden Screen: façade

proper and has been christened the Suburban Baths. The Forum Baths are of early Augustan date, with traces of later redecoration under Nero or Claudius. As usual there were two sections, one for women and a larger one for men. The entrance to the latter was in *cardo III*.

The first room is a large barrel-vaulted changing-room (*apodyterium*) with seats on three sides and long brackets divided into compartments for the clothes or bathing wraps of the clients.

On one side of this there is a small *frigidarium*, with a circular plunge, of which the blue bottom and the marine creatures painted on the vault above were designed to give the bathers a vague sensation of open space; and on the others side lay the *tepidarium*.

This too has seats and brackets and in the middle of the floor, which is raised on *suspensurae* to allow the hot air to circulate, there is a mosaic of a Triton surrounded by four dolphins.

The whole of the north side of the *calidarium* is occupied by a large hot plunge, whereas the

The Forum Baths: stucco decoration with a warrior

73

apse on the opposite side of the same room must have contained the basin (*labrum*) for washing.

The women's section, which had a separate entrance from *cardo IV,* follows the same pattern. In addition to the usual seats and brackets, the changing-room has a mosaic pavement, once again representing a Triton, this time bearing an oar on his shoulder and accompanied by a cupid, four dolphins, an octopus and a squid.

The *tepidarium*, again with seats and brackets, has a mosaic with a maeander motif framing small panels. The *calidarium* resembles, but is smaller than, that of the male section.

Behind the women's section are the furnace (*praefurnium*), together with all the arrangements for stoking and for heating the water, the service rooms, a well, and a staircase to an upper storey containing attics, a terrace and rooms for the attendants.

To the south lies the palaestra, a rectangular enclosure with porticoes on three sides and, beyond it, a large area that may have been roofed for ball-games (*sphaeristerium*).

THE SAMNITE HOUSE

First laid out in the last decades of the 2nd century B.C., this house originally occupied the whole southern part of the fifth *insula* and was only later reduced to its present size. The noble façade retains its original aspect, with a fine squared-stone doorway and Corinthian capitals. The entrance lobby is decorated in the First Style(imitating slabs of coloured marble in relief) with two Second Style landscape panels above. The Tuscan *atrium* has a concrete floor (*opus signinum*); the decoration includes an upper loggia motif with Ionic columns, a carved well-head of Hellenistic inspiration, and later, Fourth Style wall-paintings with false perspectives. The other ground-floor rooms have concrete floors and their paintings are of great delicacy.

Samnite House: the atrium

The upper storey is divided into two small apartments, one entered from outside and one from within. The latter has a balcony facing on to the street, and within it there are traces of painting and a mosaic panel with Dionysiac emblems.

THE HOUSE OF THE CARBONIZED FURNITURE

Though modest in size, this house bears the stamp of unusually cultured elegance. The *atrium* has a concrete floor and a columnar loggia like that in the Samnite House. On the right is the *triclinum*, handsomely decorated in the Fourth Style with architectural motifs and still-life panels and on the left a room with

an antechamber, which was originally a single chamber, later subdivided by a thin partition. At the back the *tablinum* has a dainty scheme of flying female figures and a large window out on to the little courtyard-garden; in the wall is the socket for a couch.

House of the Carbonized Furniture: aedicule

House of the Carbonized Furniture: painting of Dionysus

The courtyard is small and secluded. A stucco-coated *lararium* in the far wall consists of a pedimental façade carried on two columns and a recess with a shell in the apse.

Facing on to the courtyard is another room, decorated on a red ground and divided by light architectural partitions. In it were found the bed and the small table, both of excellent workmanship, which are now preserved in it, and which have given the house its name. Perhaps this too was intended to serve as a dining-room, or it may simply have been a living-room.

THE HOUSE OF POSEIDON AND AMPHITRITE

The house is grouped around a small *atrium*, in a corner of which is the base of a *lararium*. Beyond the *tablinum* is a covered dining-room, and next to it a small courtyard that is unique in the taste and quality of its ornament. The centre is occupied by a low dining-couch, faced with marble, and the walls are lavishly ornamented: on the end wall a mosaic panel of the divinities Poseidon (Neptune) and Amphitrite set in a frame beneath a spreading shell; and on the adjoining wall a nymphaeum, faced entirely in mosaic and con-

House of Poseidon and Amphitrite: mosaic panel

sisting of three niches framed between foliate and other ornamental motifs and two hunting-scenes with dogs and fleeing stags. The large shop adjoining the house and its furnishings are the best-preserved from all antiquity. In it are nearly all the fittings, large storage-jars full of foodstuffs, amphorae standing in a rack, and the counter with an openwork wooden screen behind it. In the corners are the fireplace and a large water-jar. The rooms of the upper storey too are preserved. In them can be seen traces of wall decoration, a wooden bed, a bronze candelabrum and a marble table.

THE HOUSE OF THE BICENTENARY

This house takes its name frome the fact that the clearance of it was completed in 1938, two hundred years after the excavations were begun by Charles of Bourbon in 1738. It is on of the finest houses in Herculaneum. Along the façade, on either side of the entrance there are shops, four in all, and the upper storey was bracketed out (*maenianum*). Around the spacious, but rather low, Tuscan *atrium* are the bed-chambers and the *alae* and at the far end the *triclinium* and the *tablinum*, the latter with a pavement of polychrome marble and Fourth Style paintings with mythological subjects. On two sides of the small garden beyond are porticoes, and on the other two sides a portico with windows and a large hall.

In its last phase the house underwent a number of changes. A small apartment and shop were carved out of the west side, and the upper storey was divided up into two apartments. In one of the rooms of the latter can be seen a cross-shaped impression in the white plaster, a discovery which at the time created a sensation, being widely interpreted as evidence for the spread of Christianity to Herculaneum before A.D. 79. Presently however this interpretation is being revised.

House of The Bicentenary:
exterior view

House of The Bicentenary:
det. of a painting

THE DECUMANUS MAXIMUS

The main *decumanus* of Herculaneum, the most important throuroughfare of the ancient city, had been excavated only on its upper, eastern, part.Its alignment with the structures of the important buildings that lined it, is in part visible and in part underground, but known thanks to the explorations carried out in the 1700's conducted by means of a system of shafts and galleries. Of these investigations there remain several contemporary accounts and a plan drawn at the time and published by Cocchio and Bellicard in 1754 in their book on the excavations at Herculaneum: since these are broadly confirmed by what we can now see, they can be taken as reasonably reliable.

The *decumanus* runs from east to west and is wider than the other streets of Herculaneum, with its pavements and gutter measuring about 40 feet in width, and in the part so far excavated it was unpaved. It is bordered on both sides by porticoes which lined the whole length of the street. Furthermore at its junction with *Cardo* V it was delimited by two travertine pilasters, and a tall step prevented traffic entering from *Cardo* IV. Therefore there is every reason therefore for thinking that only foot-traffic was allowed into this *decumanus* and that in this case the street served much the same function as the Forum squares of other cities. At the east end there are also traces of wooden posts such as might support temporary awnings on market days. Along the south side are large shops, patrician residences like the House of the Bicentenary, and the House of the Tuscan colums built latest at the beginning of the 1st century A.D. but modified during the imperial era with the creation, inside, of small apartments and shops, and two public buildings divided by the passageway of the *Cardo* III. The one to the east of the *cardo* can be identified with a certain degree of accuracy as the seat of the college of the *Augustales*, a religious order to

whom was entrusted the cult of the emperor: the building, built towards the end of the reign of Augustus, was already modified by his successor, Tiberius, by creating a *sacellum* at the southern end, and again under Claudius or Nero. In particular the *sacellum* is decorated by frescoes of the 4th style of the story of Hercules, the hero from whom the city took its names, and paved in *opus sectile*.The building to the west has instead been identified as the Curia, due to its looking alike that rising at the southern end of the Forum of Pompeii. Here, on the walls and in the apses there were splendid paintings (portraying Theseus and the Minotaur, Hercules and Telephus, Achilles and Chiron) and statues of marble and bronze erected in honour of various imperial personages and of members of the distinguisched and public-spirited local family of the Nonii Balbi. All of these are now in the Naples Museum. This building was very probably the Basilica, in many respects resembling in plan that of Pompeii. The structure in front of it, finely decorated with stucco coffering and figured panels, which was once believed to have been a four door arch, appears to be in fact a *chalcidicum* i.e. an ample entrance portico.

At the eastern end of the *decumanus* there is one of the monumental entryways to the Palaestra.

THE PALAESTRA

Herculaneum, like Pompeii, had a palaestra, forming a noble architectural complex at the eastern edge of the town and linked with the Decumanus Maximus and the Forum.

The Palaestra: reconstruction

In the middle of the great central open space is a cruciform pool, with a central bronze fountain in the form of a serpent with five heads entwining a tree-trunk; there is a smaller rectangular swimming pool bordering the north side. On three sides the palaestra seems to have been enclosed by porticoes, and on the fourth by a cryptoporticus. A columnar vestibule gave access from *Cardo* V, and off the east portico there opened a series of large rooms; a large hall, flanked by two smaller halls, the former with an apse and a marble pavement, and a *mensa agonistica*; a long rectangular chamber, probably a shrine of Aesculapius and Hygiaea, goddess of health; and finally a group of rooms which were accessible only from the street, and which may have been the seat of some religious or professional association connected with the athletics that took place in the palaestra. Along the north side, above the cryptoporticus, ran a long loggia for the use of spectators of the *ludi*, in particular for the magistrates and other local worthies; and behind it a series of rooms and, at the west end, a large hall, which closely resembles the lower vestibule and opens onto *Cardo* V opposite the main *decumanus*.

What survives of the wall-painting and pavements shows how rich the decoration of the individual buildings must have been. The lay-out dates from the first half of the 1st century A.D., the oldest part being the cryptoporticus. Later, under Vespasian, it underwent extensive repairs and a partial rebuilding, to repair the damage caused by the earthquake of 62.

THE HOUSE OF THE STAGS

A house in which the traditional plan has been modified to allow for the maximum of garden space within the site available. It is a relatively late building, dating from the middle of the 1st century A.D. As in the most fashionable houses the *atrium* is little more than a vestibule and is *testudinatum*, that is to say it has no central opening in the roof. Its real function was as an entrance hall giving access on the one side to a large dining-room and quadriportico, and on the other to a corridor which runs behind the dining-room to the kitchen quarter and the storerooms. In the upper storey are the slaves' rooms, with a separate wooden stair and balcony. The large dining-room is decorated with slender architectural motifs on a black ground and paved with tiles of coloured marble. The two groups of stags harried by hounds now standing in it, fine examples of Roman animal sculpture, formerly adorned the garden, together with the other small marbles that are now preserved in the house.

The garden and terrace are much larger. The dining-room and other rooms open on to a windowed corridor, in which pictures of cupids set in large red and yellow panels occupy the lower wall and a slender architectural scheme on a white ground the upper. The portico encloses a garden, at the far end of which, facing the dining-room, is a grandiose pedimental portal. This was decorated with mosaics, the surviving elements of which include a head of *Oceanus*, scrollwork, and an architrave with cupids racing on hippocamps.

House of the Stags: det. of the garden

In addition to the stags referred to above, the garden was dotted with marble tables, herms and small figures, including a drunken Hercules and a Satyr pouring wine from a skin, which closely resembles a bronze from Pompeii.

Towards the south, between the garden and the terraces, with their fine views out over the sea, there is a large hall that may have been a summer dining-room and, beside it, two smaller rooms with windows on to the garden; beyond this lies the corridor, and beyond this again there is a terrace with a central pergola and small rooms for rest and repose.

Sunken terracotta boxes were intended to hold ornamental plants and flowers.

THE HOUSE OF THE TELEPHUS RELIEF

It is a very large house; the irregularities of its plan, with rooms at different levels, are due to the exigencies of the site. In its present form the house dates from the last years of Herculaneum's existence. The *atrium* is of Corinthian type, with colonnades on three

House of the Stags: statue of the stag harried by hounds

The House of the Telephus Relief: reconstruction

sides to carry the upper walls, which in turn support the roof. Walls and columnns are painted a vivid red, and from the architraves hang carved marble *oscilla* of varied subject and shape. To the north lie the slaves' quarters, with stables, kitchen-garden and a rustic shrine. A corridor leads to a peristyle garden, between the columns of which runs a low balustrade, and in the centre a pool rendered in blue. On the south side is a group of rooms, of which the largest has a splendid pavement of shaped marble tiles and a marble wall-decoration of panels framed between spirally-fluted half-columns with Corinthian capitals. In an adjoining room was found the neo-Attic relief of Telephus from which the house takes its name.

Beneath these rooms there is a lower storey, with a large room corresponding to the hall above. This too has a marble pavement of large coloured panels within a geometrical framework; on the walls, above a marble plinth, is a painted scheme in horizontal bands, with interlace and foliate designs, birds and masks. A feature of the exterior is a façade of half-columns framing the doors and windows of an internal corridor.

THE SUBURBAN BATHS

The Suburban Baths lie in the area that began to be developed as soon as Herculaneum was free to expand outside the narrow limits of the original city. The excavation of this quarter presents many difficulties, on account both of the hardness of the rock and of the high level of the water table, and the baths are still only partly cleared. They are notable both for the logic of their plan and for the wealth of their ornament. From a large courtyard the entrance leads down into a small tetrastyle *atrium* carried on superimposed double arches; on the right is a rest-room, with large windows opening towards the sea, and in front the *apodyterium*, paved with marble slabs and equipped with a *frigidarium* plunge at the far end. Next comes a room with benches, paved in black marble and decorated in stucco with figures of warriors in high relief set in elaborate frames. To the right

lies the *calidarium*, also paved in dark marble and decorated with Fourth Style architectural stuccoes; and to the left the *tepidarium*, which is almost entirely occupied by a large marble swimming pool, the *natatio*. Beyond it lies the circular *laconicum*, or sweating-room. The plan is completed by a corridor, the furnace and various service rooms.

It will be noticed that here, unlike the other bathing establishments at Pompeii and Herculaneum, there are not two separate bathing suites, one for men and one for women.

Suburban Baths: det. of the atrium

89

Vision Publications

Series «Guides with Reconstructions»

ITALY

Rome - Past and present
Hadrian's Villa and Villa d'Este
Ostia - Past and present
Paestum - Past and present
Pompeii - Herculaneum - Past and present
Roman Catacombs and the Vatican Necropolis

GREECE

Athens - Past and present
Olympia, Mycenae, Epidauros, Corinth - Past and present
Delphi - Past and present
Ancient Crete - Past and present